THE TEENAGE WORRIER'S POCKET GUIDE TO FAMILIES

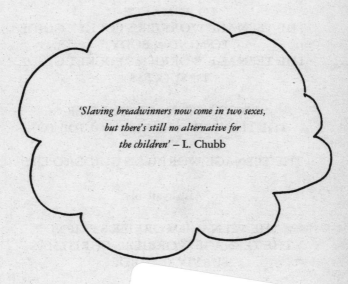

'Slaving breadwinners now come in two sexes,
but there's still no alternative for
the children' – L. Chubb

THE TEENAGE 'WORRIER'S POCKET GUIDE TO FAMILIES

Ros Asquith
as Letty Chubb

CORGI BOOKS

THE TEENAGE WORRIER'S POCKET GUIDE TO FAMILIES
A CORGI BOOK : 0 552 146420

First publication in Great Britain

PRINTING HISTORY
Corgi edition published 1998

Set in 11½pt Linotype Garamond by
Phoenix Typesetting Ilkley, West Yorkshire

Corgi Books are published by Transworld Publishers Ltd,
61–63 Uxbridge Road, Ealing, London W5 5SA,
in Australia by Transworld Publishers (Australia) Pty Ltd,
15–25 Helles Avenue, Moorebank, NSW 2170,
and in New Zealand by Transworld Publishers (NZ) Ltd,
3 William Pickering Drive, Albany, Auckland.

Made and printed in Great Britain by
Cox & Wyman Ltd, Reading, Berks.

Contents

Just a few effects of FAMILY values on a TEENAGE WORRIER...

Bed-I-had-when-I-was-seven
Miniscule Room
Matchbox Cottage
Kewforloo
Sibling by Puke
Shoe-on-Stair
Nuclear Family Wasteland
Uvverfokesox
ME 2 NOT U

Dear Teenage Worrier(s),

Does your family make you as crazy as a gerbil on tequila? Is your home that one where the phone doesn't work

a) because the company cut it off?

2) because yr big brutha's playing Pluke Nukem with a spotti-nerd in Patagonia on it? or

3) because it's superglued to yr mum's ear?

Is it that one with a lukewarm bath (always occupied by some other family member or else their horrible old flannels), a dead hairdrier and a melting fridge that only contains cans of Old Bestard lager and weird smells?

Do you watch harrowing TV documentaries about children from Tragick broken homes and think, 'Compared to my place, this is a Disney cartoon'? Do you long for FREEDOM? Or to be little again? Take heart! This handy pocket guide will steer you through the labyrinth of Family Values: Parents who are Over-protective. Parents who don't-care-are-never-there, sisters, brothers, distant

1

relatives who descend loomingly at festive seasons to remind you why you haven't seen them all year, and the constant nag, drone, hum and whirr that litters the average Teenage Worrier's home.

However packed with glume and rage home life can be, however, it is usually better than living on newspapers in a shop doorway and I intend to demonstrate (ahem) how best to make the Teenage family years bearable for all of Yooooooooooo, dearest fans, I mean readers. And hope that you may learn to embrace yr cold unwelcoming homes, with their darkened doors, both parents (if lucky enough to have same) out in bitter world struggling to make ends meet instead of caring for only offspring Etck.

SO, whether you have no blood relatives at all, came out-of-a-test-tube and want to go back, are in Care, live in a mansion or a cardboard box, are an only child or the youngest of a family of twenty — I hope there are some tips and hints to keep you smiling through your pain until, arrrrg, you are grown-up and have to face ye dread responsibilities of creating your own little nest instead.

Let me know if I have left out any searing Family-Worries so that I can add them to my next volume . . .

Lurve,

Letty Chubb

And now . . . before I begin, a brief guide to my own beloved family . . .

Mother

Forty-something, always complaining about the menopause. This is not having a pause from men, as so many women wd like, but is about when your periods start to stop and, having complained about them for years, barmy mothers start to *miss* them, mourn for lost yoof and have parties for their last tampon Etck. At least this is one Worry I can cross off my list. Phew. My only mother is still raging at my father for never making any money and I have some sympathy with her, cos she was brought up V. Rich and it must be hard to be downwardly mobile when all the gurlz at the posh skule she went to have married bank managers, werld leaders Etck, or else become same themselves. Which, since she is supposed to be a feminist, I think she shld have done. All she does is work part-time in a children's library – moaning about falling literacy standards – and pretend to paint, moaning about sacrificing her Art for her family. I don't know who this Art is, but judging by the sprouts like meteorites and unfrozen mince she gives us, he's well out of it . . .

Unconscious poetry in ye

Chubbe FAMILY

Father

To earn his pittance while slaving over his 'novel',
my briefly successful dad spends most of his time
tinkering with old machinery and taking up floors
(see **Benjy**, below). He writes about Do-It-Yourself
and, as my Only Mother frequently remarks, whilst
toiling upstairs with a bucket: 'If you live with a
plumber, your loo never flushes.' Nothing in our
house works, even the front door. Things hang off
hinges, totter at precarious angles, have gaping
holes . . . Sometimes I am surprised to find the stairs
do actually lead to the top floor. One day, my father
is bound to take them down to 'see how they work'.
The only advantage in this for *moi*, is that he is
completely uninterested in how *I* work and therefore
does not nag me daily as some V. Caring dads seem
to do. Unless, of course, I want to do anything
remotely interesting like go to the chip shop after
dark. Then it's, how far away is it? Who are you
going with? Who'll be there? (A few old trouts
absorbed in their newspapers). When will you get
back? Etck Etck. Arg.

Brother One – Ashley, 19

All of you who have written to see if handsome,
witty, caring, tall Ashley has broken up with his
fiancée can hold yr breath. There is a ray of hope, as
she has asked for a 'cooling off' period. Gasp. Ashley

is therefore currently buried under a pile of seething hopeful gurlz for whom he Does Not Care, as he has eyes only for Caroline (as do my parents, as her folks are stinking rich and they foresee one less mouth to feed Etck). Otherwise, he is going to be a doctor, save the werld Etck. And, having been my frend for years, has V. Little time for *moi*.

Brother Two – Benjy: six going on forty-five, going on two

Aaaaaaaaah. Bless. Spherical Benjy. Juggle the letters, take away a single 'l' and you have Seraphic Benjy. He may look like a cherub, but he has temper of demented hyena and strength of Hercules.

When he isn't using me as a punch-bag, trampoline, or victim of practical jokes (like offering drink from Coke bottle he's filled with mixture of marmite, washing-up liquid, sprout water, TCP and lawn food), he is climbing into my bed each night because my Only Parents are snoring too loud to hear him. It is then that I feel V. Sorry for Benjy and we both feel that Nobody Cares together.

His fear of floors, sadly, is not abating despite my father's efforts to change lino in kitchen, carpet in bedroom, mat in bathroom Etck, to suit him. Only good thing is our house is so full of junk that floors are barely visible and it is possible to skip from Lego to teddy to pile of newspapers to pile of old socks Etck and barely touch floor for years.

Granny Chubb

My dad's mum, poorer than church ant, worked
fingers to bone as cleaner and now survives on half a
tin of cat food every other Friday. Prob my favourite
person in werld, as always has big hug, loads of
time, dry biscuit and warm friendly listening face
Etck.

Granny Gosling

My mother's mother. Was V. V. V. Rich (which is
how Ashley got posh public schooling) but has hit
Hard Times. Old habits die hard though and she
still can't understand why Mr Patel at the local cash-
and-carry won't deliver champagne, truffles Etck on
credit.

Pets

Are
fleas
pets? ↗

Rover
My old faithful cat of
cats, best pal in werld
and only member of
family that truly Cares
(I think). She makes me
sneeze and wheeze and
is covered with fleas,
gets stuck up trees, but
is always pleased when

she's on my knees, that's enough eeee's please
(wonder if I could be a poet, instead of a film
director?).

Horace
Benjy's horrible gerbil – shreds paper and goes
round and round all day on wheel, just like my
Adored Father thinks people who have to work in
offices do.

Kitty
Benjy's horrible kitten wot looks sweet, has teeth
like piranha and claws like tiger and wees
everywhere.

NB Chubb family has the usual assortment of aunts,
hangers-on Etck who emerge from lairs at Christmas
to be surprised how you've grown a few inches, how
spoilt you are, how they never had computer games
in their day but made do with a handful of dried
string Etck.

And now, on with my luxurious guide to
Surviving the Family . . . and remember, dear reader,
that I still have failed to conquer my superstition
about saying that werd about dying that rhymes
with 'breath'. I always use 'banana' instead.

9

Absence

Although supposed to make Heart Grow Fonder, absence can be taken Too Far, viz: foul, unthinking parents who are out every night asking poor Teenage Worrier to babysit. Worse still is when a parent goes off altogether, saying it is better for you than hearing them fight all yr life. (What they mean is, it is better for *them* to go, because then Flossie L'Amour will stop moaning about being Just a Plaything Etck). See also DIVORCE.

Adoption

It is V. Common fantasy of Teenage Worriers to think they are adopted and, instead of being only beloved offspring of Mr and Mrs Vole, 42 Humble Gardens, Cheapside, are in fact long-lost daughter of Syd Kool, rock star, or Daphne, Princess of Zaire, Etck. Although this is V. hurtful to your only parents, if you are not adopted, it is fun to dreeeam – and why not?

In Life as it actually lived, adoption is more tricky. If you are adopted, you are bound at some stage, to wonder why your only mum gave you away to a stranger. This can lead to serious pining and feelings of being Unloved for Yourself. The reasons, however, are often V. Good and V. Complicated. Many gurlz in the past were more or less forced to give up their babies at gunpoint rather than to disgrace their families Etck and, although things are better now, there are still many people who think, if a pregnancy is unwanted, it is better to have the baby adopted than to have an abortion.

Take comfort in the fact that adopted children are usually more Lurved and wanted than the rest of us, since your Adopting Parents were so V. Desperate for a Baby they went through all that paperwork, getting references to say they were not mass murderers Etck, and even agreed to take a baby as ugly, noisy Etck as yr good self. They shld get a medal.

Hopefully, you lurve your parents and think of them (rightly) as your 'real' parents. But there will always be a nagging Worry. What was my birth mother like? What happened? Etck. As you probably know, when you are eighteen (or seventeen, in Scotland) you are allowed to find out all this stuff and if you're really sure you want to, you can try to contact your birth parents. You may, however, find that when you *do* trace your 'real' mum to her palace, or hovel, that she is V. Embarrassed or furious to see you. She may have a family of seven who she's never told, Etck Etck. NEVER JUST TURN UP. Ring or write first. And take loads of advice from adoption agency Etck.

Armchairs

The purpose of the armchair as a family member is to give all the warmth, support and comfort that your overworked uncaring parents, carers Etck do not provide.

First, it is Always There in the Same Place when you return from school.

It never minds if you want to sit on its lap.

It is softer and cuddlier than the average adult.

It never tells you off or fights back, even if you punch it.

It stays in the same place, never wandering off to the shed saying don't bother me now.

It is also more likely to find things you have lost! And to give you money! Last time I looked under our armchair cushions I found 76p in old coins (sadly, four of them had chewing-gum so firmly stuck to them that even Adored Mother's nail file wouldn't get it off).

The only V. Sad thing about armchairs is that there are never enough of them and that everyone always wants the same one. Thus, tragickly, like all other things you Lurve in life, they cause rows, arguments, glume Etck.

Aunts

My Only Mother is always groaning that aunts have it easy: they can come and pat their nieces and nephews on the head, take them out for nice trips, sweeties Etck and then swan off into distance without ever cooking meal, washing socks Etck. This is why lots of Teenage Worriers with childless aunts think their aunties are lots more fun than their poor old mums. But there are also V. Boring aunts who only ever ask you about school as if that were the most interesting thing in yr deprived and anxious Existence, and how you are doing in your exams Etck. Eeeeeek. These are the aunties who never noticed inflation, cost of living index Etck, and think you shld roll over waving yr feet in the air like joyous puppy if they give you 50p.

Babies

There are two kinds of babies. One looks like a small hairless rat, all pointy and wrinkly, the other looks like a cross between Winston Churchill, and Sir Elton John. Either kind are thought to be V. Adorable and the height of fizzical purfection Etck by their adoring mothers. BEWARE . . . this cld happen to you! Most Teenage Worriers with babies in the family, though, get them because their dad has gone off with a younger model and decided to be a better parent to his new ickle baba than he ever was to the old ones, viz YOU. Breathe deeply and try to enjoy it. V. Hard. More of this later (See STEP-PARENTS).

A new baby in the family however, is not that rare. A curious nostalgia for those sounds and smells often afflicts women of thirty-something, or even

Love is Blind dept.

forty-something, and before you know it, bang goes the computer game, trainers Etck you were expecting as there is another mouth to feed, bootees by the hearth, nappies in the bin, bottles in the fridge, crying in the night Etck, Etck.

*Moi*self, I was nearly ten when ickle Benjy was born, and I remember it well . . . The Baby bukes all said: feed baby when he wants it, and soon he shld be in a four-hour feeding pattern. A newborn will sleep about 20 hours out of 24. Huh! Benjy fed every ten minutes and slept about half an hour a day . . .

But however tiresome and drooling a baby can be, they do have a built in 'love me' factor that overrides some of the selfish yearnings even of a Teenage Worrier. Don't get one of your own until you've passed the Teenage Years though, cos you'll never be a Teenager again and they are a V. V. Big responsibility, millstone round neck Etck if they are your very own.

BIRTHDAYS

In our house, birthdays come in five different packages:

My Mother, who never tires of telling the story of how my Adored Father forgot her thirtieth birthday until he Heard her mournful little voice humming 'Happy Birthday to Me'. He was so overwhelmed with guilt about this little oversight that he has been making it up to her ever since by reminding us when her birthday is about six months before it happens. He has even been known to buy her flowers. Whatever I get her, she never notices it half as much as Benjy's cards, which he always sticks bits of old spaghetti to and writes on them: *i LuV yoo MuM, hopy birdy*, using a different colour for each letter. At the sight of this grisly edible object each year my Only Mother (who is, after all, supposed to be an *artist*) swoons and exclaims upon his massive talent. At least it's the only time she doesn't correct his spelling . . .

My Father, who always says people don't know how lucky they are. He and Granny Chubb used to sit huddled around a cheerfully crackling matchstick, taking nips from the remains of a bottle of cooking sherry she found in the neighbours' bin, while he eagerly opened his lovingly-wrapped birthday parcel containing a single sock. And glad of it.

Ashley, who opens all his presents in about five seconds, kisses everybody in about a second-and-a-half, says it's his best birthday ever and goes out of the house saying Sharon Grone round the corner has promised him something a bit special. My dad always says to bring it back we'll all have a look at it, which usually leads to an argument.

Benjy, who got up at about two in the morning on his last birthday and crashed around the house, jumping over bare patches of floor and rattling cupboard doors. He became convinced his special present was hidden in Horace's cage so he let Horace out to investigate and then trod on him in the dark, concluding to his horror that the floor had turned into warm, squeaking wriggly stuff, and yelling so that lights went on all down the street. Adored Mother now plans to give Benjy two spoonfuls of Kalpol at bedtime before his next birthday, but it will just mean he will get up at three instead of two and fall downstairs.

Rover gets up on her birthday, stretches, rips up carpet, sofa Etck, hisses at Granny Chubb's slippers, slops milk on floor, has choking fit trying to eat Fatto Catto too fast, walks haughtily past hopeful looking brand-new toy mouse with ribbon tied round tail donated by El Chubb, and goes back to sleep. Rover's birthdays do not stand out like pyramids of Fatto Catto in her calendar I feel.

Did I say five? Of course, there is also the humble birthday of **moi**, but that, dear reader, is just like yr own. A long slow yearning, a fever of anticipation, a slow deflation (sounds V. like sex might be) as exciting parcel turns out to be puce and mustard bolero, wrong CD, Improving Buke, Etck. There is always a card from relative saying get yrself something lovely, with paperclip (but no money) attached, *no* card from true lurve Etck. And there is

An embroidery Kit!
My cup runneth over!

Embroider Your Cushions

always a note of sadness in among the pleasure. No bloom without gloom, sez El Chubb. On each birthday, I always find one small bit of it goes slowly, spent yearning for my lost yoof, for when days were long and full of play, when parties were just about playing pass the parcel and being sick into your best frend's jelly. Now parties are a hive of seething Worries about who's snogging who? Who's wearing what? Who's there, who's not . . .

z z z z Z z z z z

Rover does not bother about parties

Brothers

My readers will know I have two of these items: a Saint and a Nutcase. Living up to one (impossible) and down to the other occupies great swathes of El Chubb's psyche and most gurlz with brothers will have similar probs to mine:

Brothers: get bigger helpings, even when they're smaller.

Brothers: are often covered from head to foot in mud but no-one seems to mind.

Brothers: play lots of shooting games, even in houses that don't buy toy guns.

Brothers: need their confidence building up, because boyz are falling behind gurlz . . . er, when I luke at Big Werld, I see no sign of Women running it.

Brothers: have Obsessions: football, computer games, Lego, floors . . .

Brothers: are allowed to stay up later, go out more, play music louder, not tidy up, never wash up, often don't wash at all.

So much for the march of feminism. When I moan to my Only Mother about her principles of Equality she goes V. red and says she can't be bothered to nag them all day. Why can she be bothered to nag *me* all day then?

NB Teenage Worriers with sisters have same probs, joyz Etck as far as I can see, except they borrow yr clothes more. See SISTERS.

CARE

There is a Thingy yr life can be ruined by now – it is a dysfunctional family. The newspapers are full of it, viz: the Royal family is dysfunctional, Etck. But what it means to children in a really dysfunctional family in real Life, not palaces and nannies Etck, is that they are Put Into Care. The contradiction in putting kids 'In Care' is that it often means the exact opposite: social workers take them away from violent bullying drunk abusive parent and put them into Children's Homes where they are at risk of being abused, bullied Etck by complete strangers instead. Not surprisingly, most children prefer the Devil-they-know. But despite all the horrible things that can happen to kids, there *are* decent people out there who are longing to foster or adopt. If your own parent or carer is cruel or abusive in any way, it is V. Important to discuss it with someone outside yr home. A teacher or yr doctor, or even a V. Close frend. Try V. hard to get help.

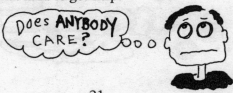

CHORES

old socks are everywhere

Chore Tips

Despite own household being lost cause, here are a few ways for Normal Teenage Worriers to negotiate chore-nagging:

1) Make parent or carer a cup of tea now and then. Once-yearly is about enough for them to think you are a Caring, sharing person.
b) Stuff socks Etck in drawer once a month.
C) When cutting crusts off bread, put them in bin. Better still, put them out for little birdies.
4) Eat straight out of fridge, to avoid plate-washing.
e) Try to remember to close fridge door.
6) Cook family meal now and then. Again, once yearly is often enough. It is also often enough to listen to chorus of praise afterwards: eg: 'It's lovely when you cook, darling, but every surface is covered with what seems to be glue and fluff? Part of cooking is also cleaning up, sweetheart.' (Or words to that effect.)

YES! An elderly sock!

mould

What DO they teach them at school dept?

CUDDLY TOYS

Family Life is not complete without army of cuddly toys given at various sentimental occasions so that each of them reminds you of sad or happy moment viz: giant penguin my father gave my mother on her thirtieth birthday. Or, old teddy, rabbit, fur budgie Etck you had when you were one. Or, puce frog you won at fair when you were eight and have carried in yr pocket ever since but never admitted to anyone. Occasionally you pull it out, by mistake, stuck to a piece of old gum and then you explain that it belongs to yr baby brother.

DADS

If you are lucky enough to have yr dad living with you (see DIVORCE, ORPHANS Etck) and he is reasonably kind Etck you will still have plenty to mone about. This is because to mone, grone, and be filled to brim with glume at Yuniverse is part of the lot of all Teenage Worriers and to occasion these noises is part of the lot of all dads. Here are a few types of dad. If yours is not here, please send him to me in large brown envelope and I will try and include him in next buke (yeeech).

Big Daddy

This is the V. Successful, striving, world conquering Dad. He is V. Big at work, with thrusting car, wallet, Etck. When you were little you were V. Proud of him cos of all the V. Clever things he did. But you cld hardly remember

what he looked like, cos you were in bed when he got home and he left house before you woke up. Mr Big goes to lots of conferences at weekends, so you didn't see much of him then, either. You can remember at least four birthdays where he couldn't show up . . . (sound of violins, wail of bansheees Etck.)

Now you are a Teenage Worrier, he finds you much more interesting, inviting you to go with him to parties Etck. Sadly, you are not V. Keen on his frendz, life, werk. And he is V. V. V. not keen on all of yours. He has sent you to a posh skule, but wonders why he wasted the money since all you do is hang out with skinheads/hippies/rastas Etck. This kind of DAD is known as *work-rich, time-poor.*

Little Daddy

This is the kind of daddy
it can be hard to be
anything other than V.
Small with yrself. When

you were an ickle baba he seemed like a Big Daddy
because he was bigger than you, anyway. As you got
older you realized people often turned the lights out
and went out of the room while he was still in it,
gave him lots of V. Boring werk to do that he was
too nervous of The Sack to mone about (except at
home), pushed in front of him in kews, mistook him
for a twig, roll of lino, small wrinkly ornament
Etck. However, no-one lurves this kind of Daddy
like his own family, thank goodness, and lurve prob
keeps his werld going round.

Bad Daddy

Drinks, chases women Not His Wife, drives too fast,
calls people he crashes into Blind, Morons Etck,
responds to complaints that He's Not Being Fair
with 'life's not fair', shouts, tells people criticizing
his bad habits Not To Give Him A Hard Time
Etck. Often had Bad Daddy himself. If you are
unlucky enough to have this kind of Daddy, you
may still be able to reach his Heart sometimes (most
people have one somewhere) but don't depend on it
lasting.

Let's <u>hope</u> this kind of DAD is going out of fashion...

Cross Daddy

Criticizes rather than shouts, doesn't drink (though it might help), thinks everything you do is a sign you're Not Trying. Like Bad Daddy, this type often had to deal with the same kind of stuff when they were little, and so are just passing it on. Trust yr own sense of what is Fair and what isn't. If yr daddy is cross because you haven't done something you promised to, or lied, or risked yr neck for something daft, think about saying Sorry. If yr Daddy is cross for no reason, it may be a one-off. If he's cross all the time fr nothing, enlist support from other members of yr family, and tell him you're a person too.

Dreaming Daddy

There is a DREAMER in Each one of us

Not a bad Daddy as they go, but it can get V. Annoying, espesh if you want to do most of the Dreaming around the house yrself. Dreaming Daddy is bored by the werld of shopping lists, gerbil food, MOT tests, mixer-taps, dirty washing, moneing humanity, rubbish bags Etck, and who isn't? Shout in his ear once in a while to let him know you're still there.

Perfect Daddy

I know my own Adored Father isn't purrfect, but I don't know any of my Frendz who've got a Perfect Daddy either, at least to hear the way they talk about it. Maybe they don't exist, but I can tell you what my Perfect Daddy might be like:

1) V. Handsome and Witty, so all my Frendz think he's Kule.

2) V. Decent and Honourable, so that he doesn't reckon any of the people who think he's Handsome and Witty wld be more Fun than his Adored Spouse, Family Etck.

* 3) Rich. No explanation necessary. (see above)

4) Nobel Prizewinner. Virtue of this as (1), but also for generating V. Proud feeling that he is helping to Save Werld Etck. Also superior brane-power may be in genes, rub off on offspring Etck.

5) Listening/Understanding — doesn't mind clothes sodden with tears of Teenage Worriers, wails of Nobody Cares Etck. When you're telling him How You Feel, doesn't interrupt, or say I Felt The Same At Yr Age, or paraphrase what you just said to mean something Completely Different.

Mad Daddy

Can be quite closely related to Bad Daddy and Cross Daddy, or suffer from delusions all the way from believing the world will discover their Genius one day (which is qu. normal) to thinking they're Napoleon and trying to direct the traffic in Slugg's

Lane to outflank the traffic in Ferret Cuttings
(which is not). Only if 1) it's behaviour that is
upsetting or hurting you, the family or anyone else,
or 2) you observe what seems to you V. Weird Stuff
going on over a long time and getting worse, shld
you Worry about it. The borderline between
eccentrick behaviour and madness is a narrow one
and sometimes only our Lurved Ones care about us
enough to know we're crossing it.

Divorce

Families need fathers, goes the old saying, as zillions
of single Mums trail to family support agencies Etck
attempting to get their offspring's dads to pay up
some dosh towards their bootees, nappeees, Etck. For
many of them it is tragick losing battle, so the Govt
is now keen for them to go out to work so their only
children see even less of them as well as not having a
dad around. Ho-hum. El Chubb sez: *Kidz need parents*!

And Teenage Worriers need them even more than
ickle babas, cos it's us lot that have to cope with
steaming mean streets full of drug-dealers Etck and
need cosy refuge, hot water bottle, listening ear Etck
which most parents are too busy to provide as it is. If
you have no parents you will certainly know what I
mean. So it is V. V. Hard, if you have been used to
having yr mum and dad around, to find that they
have actually chosen to separate.

Fact is, the nuclear family unit is a V. Rocky little boat, tossed on stormy seas, and vast amounts of tolerance are needed for ancient couple to stay together through thin and thick. But let's hear it for the kids! Did we ask to be born? Er, who knows? Probably we did. We were probably whirling about in space trying to get into heaven and being told, 'Go away, you've got to live 80 more lives yet before you're worthy of getting in on level one!' 'Oh, OK' we muttered, 'I'll go and find some Earthly parent then, and have another go.' And off we slouched, wings in pockets, kicking cosmic dust. Who knows?

I think it is always best to say how you REALLY FEEL. Of course, this will make them feel much more guilty even than your stiff upper lip Etck but at least it will:

a) possibly help them to come to some better arrangement (like seeing Flossie Scroggins every third Thursday, or only going out with Dominic L'Amour on Valentines Day)

b) or at least help them to respect your feelings and talk to you like an adult.

All this is V. Important, as Teenage Worriers spend a lot of time and energy on worrying how their parents are feeling and being V. Guilty cos their mother is in tears, on Prozac, or their father is drinking himself into an early banana Etck and they think it's their fault. Your parents' problems are NOT your fault. However V. Bad you think you might have been, you have NOT caused them to

31

separate (poss exception in case of Benjy, whose floor phobia does threaten family home).

If your parents already have divorced, you may well find compensations: eg: two homes to go to, lots more attention due to their guilt, V. kind step-parents Etck. All this, it must be said, can definitely be better than living with two adults who can't stand the sight of each other and are only staying together cos of you. And the biggest compensation of all, in a time of family breakdown, is knowing you are NOT ALONE.

Dummies

← wld like one of these moiself

If there's a baby in yr house, I V. Much hope there is also a dummy. They are V. Nice sucky things that give loads of comfort to ickle babas and also to their ickle mums who wld be going up wall otherwise at sound of baba yelling house down.

Embarrassment

Would adult dummies stop parents smoking?

Where to begin? As if the life of a Teenage Worrier wasn't embarrassing enough already, the Family rears its many bespectacled head to embarrass you at every opportunity. They SING, loudly, out-of-tune, V. Naff old songs at the supermarket check-out, just as you are languidly pretending to be shopping-alone, and eyeing-up Alfonso Dreamboat in the adjoining queue. They wear horrible scruffy clothes at parents' evenings and loudly boast about how they smoked 'a bit of dope themselves and it-didn't-do-them-any-harm' in front of yr head teacher!

Or V. Distant relatives wave the last picture of you they got, which was you naked, aged two, in a paddling pool IN FRONT of yr frendz . . .

Or they insist on phoning you at a party!

Or coming to pick you up from same cos it's after 8.30 p.m!

Or they make you wear a hat! Just cos there's a bit of snow!

Or buy you some grotty coat with a fur collar!

Or insist you wear gloves even if the only ones in the house have pink hippos on them!

Or, they knit you lime green and puce scarves . . . (I always slip on the one Granny Chubb knitted for me just as I go in her door, she can still make out the colours and it is a V. Small sacrifice to see her face light up with the joy of recognition).

FOSTERING

If there is serious trouble at home or yr folks are dead or in jail, you may well be fostered by some lurving person who makes jam sponges and is always home when you get back from skule. Foster-parents are checked out by local authorities Etck and, since they are actually offering to look after children rather than having to cope with result of burst condom Etck like so many 'real' parents, are often much better at it. Although there are bad foster-parents, the vast majority of them are V. Caring, and, if you become V. Happy with them, you may stay a long time, although fostering is usually temporary until you get back with your own flesh'n'bludde.

The family we all dream of, Noble Dad who earns fortune yet still has time to make moon rocket, buy designer trainers Etck and Noble Mum who earns fortune but is Always There For You exist only in fantasy. But if you've got just one adult who is a weeny bit like either of these, count blessings Etck (writhe, guilt, must practise what I preach Etck).

Garden

A garden is a place for ye familye to gather in Spring for egg-hunts, Summer for lazy barbecues, Autumn for bonfires, Winter for snowfights. Or so it goes in ye dreame family picture buke we all keep in our heads. This garden is big, with climbing frames, tree houses, pools Etck. True Life reveals few paradises such as these.

Grandparents

Tales at Granny's Knees.

In El Chubb's Dream Yuniverse, every Teenage
Worrier wld be blessed with a full set of four
grandparents and a couple of great grannies cackling
in the corner, *comparing dentures*, and wittering on
about how sweet the Teenage Worrier is, how well
they remember their own Teenage years, how
naughty they were themselves *holding hands without
contraception, smoking behind bike shed* Etck, how they
wld love to be young again but how nice it is to see
young people enjoying themselves Etck and
wouldn't they like a nice hot mug of cocoa Etck.

Real life, tragickally, sees that you are dead lucky if
you've got one grandparent living and I realize I am
V. Lucky to have two grannies (sadly, both grandpas
popped their clogs before I was a twinkle in anyone's
eye), and both are living in this country, but . . .

Granny Gosling is not a V. Perfect model. It is V.
Difficult to think of anything to say to her, even in
thank-you letters. If you don't write on the day you
receive her present she will be on the phone to your
aged anxious parent quick as a whippet to enquire if
you have suffered Tragick Accident or if you are
simply Ye Ungrateful Pigge Etck. If you *do* write,
she will go as follows, viz: 'Goodness, Scarlett!
You've discovered the application of the exclamation
mark! But have you never encountered the comma,
or the virtues of understatement?'

Granny Chubb, however, is model for all that is
purrfect about human Nachure Etck. Poor but
happy, she has the most valuable thing that anyone

37

can give a child, or a Teenage Worrier. And that is: TIME. I know I can drop round to Granny Chubb's sparkling hovel at any time of ye day or night and she will be there with willing smile, stale dog biscuit and freshly knitted bolero for *moi*. She is clean and good and bright and honest as day is long. I V. Much hope, that with her example shining before me like bright starre, I will be able to become like her too one day. And, *IT'S NOT FAIR* that she can't afford one decent pair of specs when Granny Gosling has three pairs.

Holidays

A time of joy and family bonding, when you can cast off cares of werk and skule and splash happily in ocean or laze by pule Etck, thinking happy thoughts of lurve for each other and having V. Nice REST. If yr family holiday doesn't sound quite like this, don't despair. Most people get on worse on holiday than at any other time of year. This is because all the routine things that keep you going are stripped away and you are confronted with: EACH OTHER. Aargh, yeech, giveusabreak Etck.

Small impression of average family holiday
WEATHER CONDITIONS

HOME

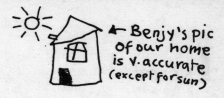

← Benjy's pic of our home is V. accurate (except for sun)

'Home sweet home'. 'Home is where the heart is' 'There's no place like Home'. It may be that cos we have all grown up with cute slogans like this lighting up in neon cross-stitch inside our brains, that our homes are usually so V. Disappointing. It is a big part of all yuman nachure to Dream and almost the whole part of a Teenage Worrier's nachure. But while ten-yr-old boyz and thrusting adults with bulging wallets Etck dream of mansions and parkland and helicopter pads, Teenage Worriers are looking for something more simple. This simple thing is called: *cosy.* Cosy could be a mat that says WELCOME. Cld be a real coal fire. Cld be just knowing there'll be a light on and something in the fridge. Being cosy is about feeling welcomed and comfy, feeling there's a big fat cushion to curl up on, a picture on the wall you have looked at all yr life, a couple of books in the bookcase that have always been there . . . If you are lucky enough to come Home to somewhere comfy and even luckier to find your mum or dad or other caring adult humming over a hot meal, you are lucky indeed. Sadly, many middle-aged worriers spoil this possible bliss by yelling 'Do your homework/oboe practice/thank-you letter' Etck the minute poor exhausted Teenage Worrier walks in the door.

INCEST

Do not confuse with incense. Incest is something that smoulders all right, but not on a dish in the corner, so don't go into the house of Abigail Knotte, the hippy yoga teacher down the road and say 'what a nice smell of incest'. Incest is sexual activity between members of the same family, *but* unlike when yr baby brother first hears about sex and asks if he can try it with you, it is about akshul activity. If anyone in yr family EVER touches you in a way you don't like, or suggests something that is your 'little secret' that makes you feel creepy, get help fast. They need help too, but you need it more. When something like this happens, Boyz and Gurlz often think they are the only person who it is happening to, and they feel too scared to say anything and suffer sometimes for years. Often they can feel guilty, as though it's their fault, or they led the adult on or even that they enjoyed it a bit. But it is NOT their fault, ever, it is ALWAYS the adult's fault and no adult shld ever ever make sexual advances to a child. Neither shld a step-parent make advances, even if you are sixteen. Yr home shld be a place of safety from all this, so you HAVE to tell. If there is no-one you trust enough to tell, ring CHILDLINE (see numbers at end of buke) and they will give you advice in confidence.

INDEPENDENCE

One of the V. Difficult things about being a Teenage Worrier, is that you want to do everything, all the time, be completely free of yr family, have no guilt or responsibility, stay up till 2 a.m. dancing every night Etck and, at exactly the SAME TIME, you want to curl up in front of telly with hot choccy watching yr Mum knit bedsocks. But how can you prove to your parents that you can now tie own shoelaces, catch bus, walk straight line (pref. not under bus) Etck? Poor frantick parents are sure that wild drugges are coursing through the veins of their beloved offspring, and that old men in dirty macintoshes are waiting to leap upon helpless Gurlz beneath every broken street lamp.

So to convince yr parents you are going to be V. Sensible, read a V. Good guide on drugs, tell your folks you know all about them and exactly what to do if you are offered any, recite Green Cross Code, declare you will not go off in strangers' car Etck and then put foot firmly out of door, telling frantick elder when you will return. If you get back five mins before the time you say for the first dozen times you go out, frantik elder will breathe huge sigh of relief, assume you are responsible (we hope) and then the werld am your oyster. On V. Cold rainy nights when all you want is aforesaid telly and hot choccy Etck

41

your old folks will prob start asking why don't you go out more? Haven't you got any frendz? Etck. So you can't win.

IT'S NOT FAIR

NO, it's NOT (see quarrels)

Most common three words in English language. El Chubb's department of statistics show that these three werds are spoken 497 times more each day than those other three that you long to hear from lips of belurved Etck. Other close contenders are: 'I didn't do it' and 'It's not my fault'.

JOKES

Ho Ho Ha Ha He He

Family jokes are Stuff of Life and V. good glue for sticking Members of Unit back together again after quarrels Etck. Being butt of family jokes is, however, not gratest fun in world. 'Ho ho ho' chortle vast throng of relatives as you walk past, mystified, with 'Reduced to Clear' sign stuck on yr back. 'Sorry, Sharon's a bit tied up at the moment' sez hysterical older Brutha on phone to Greatest Lurve of Life as you struggle to untie yr shoe-laces from table-leg Etck.

April Fools jokes are other V. Jolly family things that V. Jolly family types love to chortle at, at yr expense. Benjy's favourite is to say Rover has been

Ha Ha Ho Ho Ha Ha Ho Ho Ha Ha Ho Ho

run over. This is not my idea of fun. It doesn't
matter that I check the calendar for months before
April Fools' day. I still forget, every time. However,
V. Easy to pay him back with practical joke, ie:
bowl of custard by bedside so he steps straight in it
on waking. Sadly, if I do such a thing, I suffer for
days. 'Scarlett!' (my mother using my full name is
V. Big Warning Sign) 'How could you! Poor Benjy!
You KNOW he's scared of floors! You're old
enough to know better.' Etck. Etck. Yawn. So much
for family fun.

V.Unkind April Foole joke
perpetrated on moi last year...

KITCHENS

YES! THOSE
SOCKS
are
BACK

← crumbs

My mother's dream kitchen is like those ones you
get dragged round on school visits to olde stateley
homes Etck. Huge, clanking with pots the size of
dustbins hanging from the ceiling, and strange
pulleys, pestles, epistles Etck, throbbing with cooks,
chefs, under-butlers, housemaids all bobbing and
blushing and saying 'yes m'am' – a haven that she
only has to breeze into with the week's menu and a
condescending smirk. As it is, she blames her
inability to cook anything but over boiled sprouts
on the pre-War gas cooker my Only Father
inherited from Granny Chubb. This is not a V.
Successful ploy since my Only Father's memories of
his mum's home-cooking are wreathed in the aroma
of fresh-baked apple pies, mountains of cloudy
mashed potato fluffier than a flock of sheep Etck.
Granny Chubb provided all this food for my father
and his horde of siblings on the wages of a cleaner,
so why can't my mother do better? Depending on
my mood, I take whichever side suits *moi* best, ie:
Mother's side (feminist line): If you don't like it, cook
it yourself. *Father's side*: Who mends the plumbing,
wiring, takes up floors Etck? You expect me to cook
as well?

Ye Kitchen is a sanctuary in some homes: cosy
country-style range, kettle on hob Etck, smiles on

faces of occupants conceived by top designers, gleaming American-style worktops, scrubbed pine tables, fresh bunch of flowers, blah. Ours is more like war zone from *Newsnight*: V. Small formica-topped table covered in cigarette burns and coffee rings, ancient sink with permanently dripping tap, stove as above, miniscule fridge with ice compartment big enough for half fishfinger, drawers that won't open until pulled right out so all cutlery (three pieces) clangs on floor. Fetid hygiene-free cupboards crammed with broken pans, fine layer of volcanic ash covering everything . . .

TIPS AND HINTS FOR SMOOTHLY FUNCTIONING TEENAGE WORRIER'S KITCHEN LIFE

marrows? or socks?

I know many of my readers will be blessed with fancy gadgets like microwaves, freezers, dishwashers, coffee makers Etck, but for those of you like me, for whom the 20th century seems to have passed your parents by, there are ways of making kitchen life relatively stress-free:

1) After meal, scrape remains off plate and into bin. Leave plate to soak in lukewarm water (use it hot, if it werks) to avoid burnt chicken nugget Etck becoming eternally fused to plate.

2) Always wipe surfaces after meal, espesh surfaces of Yrself. Your sleeve will do, if, as in our home, you can never find cleanish dish cloth.

3) If you can't be bothered to wash up, eat straight

out of fridge by a) inserting head into fridge (fine on Summer mornings) or b) taking handfuls of food from within, using fingers.

Loo paper

← DON'T let a PUPPY near YOURS

Keep a roll in yr room. It is the only way of ensuring you have some when you need it. As my mother is fond of saying: 'I'm always buying rolls of loo paper, but it just gets USED UP'. This is undeniable. If it were not being used up, one dreads to think what the outcome wld be, though one cld possibly charge admission to house for all those curious to savour the ambiance of Life In The Middle Ages During Ye Plague. What does she *expect* us to do with it? Admire its noble, rounded form?

Love

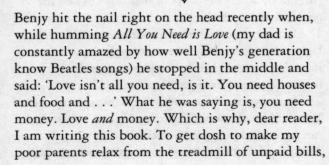

Benjy hit the nail right on the head recently when, while humming *All You Need is Love* (my dad is constantly amazed by how well Benjy's generation know Beatles songs) he stopped in the middle and said: 'Love isn't all you need, is it. You need houses and food and . . .' What he was saying is, you need money. Love *and* money. Which is why, dear reader, I am writing this book. To get dosh to make my poor parents relax from the treadmill of unpaid bills,

46

crazy schemes for selling off one room of the house Etck Etck.

One of the first tasks of the Teenage Think Tank shld be to think up new alternatives to the family. But, I must confess that your family are the only ones you can rely on to lurve you more or less whatever you do and even though they criticize you night and day, you know they will stand by you in the end. It may be that money can buy you out of lots of family responsibilities and that rich loveless households lead to white-collar crime that never gets found out whereas poor loveless families lead to jail, but still, you do need the lerve, more than the money.

Probably the best test of lurve is to say: If a ten-ton block of concrete were poised above my (*insert brother, sister, auntie or whoever in this space*), would I feel worried that it wld crush them or worried that it wouldn't? Hmmm . . .

MEAL-TIMES

I have a fantasy breakfast. I've seen it on TV. It's where an all-American Mom with smile designed by Interior Decorating firm (see KITCHENS) says in a lilting, sing-song voice, 'Come on down kids, bagels and cream cheese!' Right on cue, down come the Perfect Family: Lucinda, 17, pink cheeked and blonde, Ricky, 12, a bundle of cheerful exuberance, with a cheeky baseball cap tilted back and a ready joke for all; and cute little Mary-Lou, seven, in a flowered pinafore and bunches. 'Oh wow, Mom! Bagels!' they happily cry, as tall, lean, smiling Pop in jeans saunters in, arms full of oranges the size of California and squeezes them oh so freshly into a jug the size of The Universe. The Perfect Family may follow up with flapjacks, waffles and maple syrup, fresh fruit salad of mango and guava, before moving in an orderly fashion to a Tonka Toy 4x4 the size of a tank for their leisurely mountain drive to school.

Breakfast in *our* house sees my mother, on the rare occasions she is up, mournfully burning toast, shaking empty cornflakes packets and demanding why no-one but her ever does any shopping. My Only Father, when in paternal mood, will often spend the precious ten minutes of breakfast family-time, cutting the crusts of Benjy's toast or trying to make him a dinosaur-shaped peanut butter sandwich. If you have ever tried cutting white sliced bread with a dinosaur-shaped pastry cutter, you will have realized that the trampoline type texture of same leads to langwidge unsuitable for a family buke or to the casualty dept. Father alternates this gentle, see-what-I'll-do-for-my-children mode with a droning rant along the lines that he walked ten miles to school and back with a handful of hot gravel Etck and we don't know how spoilt/lucky/selfish/self-centred/grasping/self-indulgent/greedy Etck we are. Greedy! Huh! I

Bagels! ♥
Maple Syrup...
PANCAKES!
Eggs $unny side up!
Freshly Squeezed
Guava Juice

One flaked corn
Drop of 4-day old
Milk.
Burnt crumb of toast
(at least soot conceals mould)

hurtle out of house with only one flaked corn in my poor lonely stomach, the wails of Benjy ('Not well! Not feel like school! Gonna be sick!') in my ears and only the dread knowledge that my PE kit is still pursuing its dreary journey going round and round in washing machine and therefore will give me an excuse to miss PE, to comfort me. So much for quality breakfast-time.

As for Sunday Lunch, wot used to be family occasion round roast beef Etck, there is now only glumey fumes of burning pot noodle since half family is vegetarian, quarter are suffering assorted food phobias and rest are at pub. Dream teas are no longer either . . . El Chubb longs for thinly sliced cucumber sarnies and choccy biscuits on fine bone china Etck, when she returns from skule . . . (sob).

Mums ♡! ♡?

Like Dads, Mums come in many forms. They have to be pretty disgraceful for most Teenage Worriers not to care about them at all though, so if you are really horrible to yr mum, ask yrself, does she deserve this? Your conscience will be yr guide. Do you, though, deserve what *she* is doing to you? Ask HER that – and her conscience will be *her* guide. Saying 'I only want the best for you' Etck simply isn't gude enough. Of course she does. And so do you. One of most frequent choruses from mothers is:

'I only want you to be Happy'. How helpful is that? How do you get to be Happy anyway? And can you ever be happy enough for your mum?

Here are a few types. If your mum isn't here, please send her to me so I can include her in next buke.

Career Mummy

V. Successful, striving, werld conquering Mum. Like Big Daddy, she is V. Big at werk, with thrusting car, wallet, mobile phern Etck, but unlike Big Daddy she usually finds Handover to Au Pair at crack of dawn and return to resentful, whingeing offspring minutes before Bedtime harder to handle.

Just the same, she had to go to lots of conferences at weekends when you were little, on trips to New York to clinch Deal of Ye Century Etck, so you didn't see much of her. You can remember at least four birthdays where she couldn't show up . . . (sound of violins, wail of banshees Etck.)

Now you are a Teenage Worrier, she finds you both more interesting and possibly unfair competition because you are a disconcerting reminder that she is not getting any younger. Unlike Big Daddy, she is less likely to invite you out with her, espesh if you are going through Luminous Waif phase.

Self-Pitying Mummy

This is the kind of mummy who is always saying everything is Her Fault and, in a way that makes everybody feel they've got an itch they can't scratch, seems to be suggesting it's Their Fault Too, for being happier than she is. Like Horace, she goes round and round on a wheel, and the wheel seems to keep getting smaller and her with it. She can't Take Her Mind Off Things At Home By Going Out And Doing A Little Job Because Who'd Have Her At Her Age? She Doesn't Know How To Do Anything/Her Back Hurts/There's Nowhere To Park/She can't Have A Fling because She's An Old Bag/Your Father's A Jerk But I Can't Hurt Him/Sex Destroys Women/She can't Join A Book Group Because The Hamster Needs Feeding in the Evenings Etck Etck.

However, no-one lurves this kind of Mummy like her own family, thank goodness, and Lurve probly keeps her wheel going round. If you detect any similarities with Little Daddy, it is not coincidental.

Naughty Mummy
Drinks.

This, sadly, is often the Main Prob with Naughty Mummy. She may also Watch Telly Too Much/Play Bingo/Do The Lottery/Run Amok With the Creditcard/Flirt Past The Embarrassment Threshold/Wear Clothes that make Madonna look like Mother Teresa. This kind of Naughty Mummy is Doing The Best She Can, and doesn't realize people see it differently.

Naughty Mum always did believe in a mix of
Breast and Bottle...

NB Naughty Mummy is often seen by World as Respectable citizen.

Nagging Mummy

Like Cross Daddy, is driven by Compulsion that nobody's ever trying, espesh their Own Offspring. But in Nagging Mummy case, frustrated rage and sarcasm assisted by Eyes-To-Heaven disbelief that she cld have brought into the world someone so Totally Stoopid, Inept and unaware of Glorious-Role-in-Life as Yrself.

Like Cross Daddy, this type often had to deal with all this from their own Parents when they were little, and are passing it on with interest, in every

54

sense of the Werd. However, as with Cross Daddy, there may be a point to all this — if yr mum does not usually go on like this, you may Yrself have provided Straw That Breaks Camel's Back by yr own slobbishness, forgetfulness, unawareness that yr Mum is Also A Person Quite Like You Etck. However, if Yr Mum constantly nags, she may be unhappy, and you may be able to help her figure out why. Nagging can begin with many things, from concern that a Lurved One is Blowing It, to concern that a Lurved One is Making It The Way You Wished You Had, or Not Being The Only Kind of Person It's Worth Being and you have to Listen Hard to work out which is which.

Vague Mummy
Lurves visits to Nat Gallery to marvel at True Art, may even be in Lurve with True Art but married to miserable, sloshed, slovenly Unreliable Bert.

Like Dreaming Daddy, a Prob if you want to monopolise the *Mooning About In Dream State* department. But Vague Mummies are also Lurveing, because they believe that Yumans Falling On Each Other In Helpless Amazement is what's really happening, and anything other that that is just going to go down the pan at the Final Judgement. Tend to like blokes with V. Long Curly Hair, a throwback to 19th century poets Etck, who strode about in woodlands Etck thanx to allowances from rich relatives. Heart in Right Place, however.

Mad Mummy

As with Dads, can be qu. closely related to related categories. May shout all the time, curl up in corners In Despair, drink. May be completely normal person Driven To Limit. May hear voices, feel driven to commit violent or self-destructive act, feel werthless Etck, in which case urgent help is necessary. If Yr Mum thinks she is Boadicea, who almost repulsed the Roman invaders singlehanded driving only a horse-drawn Nissan Micra with sharp bits on the wheels, this may be merely a self-affirming fantasy that will pass, or she may be Totally Barking. As with Mad Daddy, I wld say the key factors are whether you feel personally distressed and oppressed by her behaviour, or whether you come to the conclusion that even the most broadminded person you know would reckon she is hanging perilously over the edge of Normal Behaviour. Families can be bad judges of this, because they're all in it together and the decline can be unnoticeable. Talk to yr closest friends, or even yr teachers and doctor.

Perfect Mummy

As readers will know, I am not afraid to call *moi*self a feminist. I am a firm believer in ye equality of ye sexes, but when I compare my idea of the Perfect Mummy, with the Purrfect Daddy above, I find some telling differences. I feel this shld give rise to sober contemplation on nature of Yuniverse Etck, but is prob more to do with ye slowly shifting roles and expectations. Our mother's generation was not equal to our father's, in treatment, or in expectation. And we treat them differently too. How will it be for us and our kids? I cannot help wondering . . .

SO: a Perfect Mummy, *moi* thinks, cld be any one of the types I have listed here, just so long as she's *your* Mum. Perfect Mummy shld always be free for a hug, always be ready to listen, be as happy as poss with her Own Life so she can let you be as Happy as poss with yours. She shld give you advice when you ask for it, but try not to when you don't. This doesn't sound like a lot, but it seems like it is . . .

MUSIC

Can be V. Exhausting in families cos once you get more than two people in a room you get more than one kind of music being demanded . . . Our 'living' room often resounds to Radio 3 (my mother, harking back to classical music of early childhood, which wafted across rolling lawns crammed with ponies, groom Etck), *Teddy Bears Picnic* (Benjy's plastic record-player he had when he was two, which he still carries wherever he goes), Blind Willy Lemon's trumpet (Ashley is big jazz fan) and the excellent taste of *moi*, Letty Chubb, with my up-to-the-minute-state-of-the-art-newer-than-new Chumbawamba. 'Turn it down!' shouts my Only Father, unable to concentrate on his Heavy Metal.

'Which one?' we innocently reply.

Some Teenage worriers mone and drone about how their horrible parents force them to practise their violins, oboes Etck. They do not know how lucky they are (sob). Tragickly, my own familye never made us do any of that, so my latent talent as grate musician will be for ever under wraps. And since music and all ye arts are V. Underfunded and nobody on National Curriculum cares, most of my frendz at Sluggs have never tinkled the ivories Etck. Campaign for FREE MUSIC LESSONS (V. Good for soul).

NANNIES

Work-rich and time-poor parents salve their consciences by spending hard-earned dosh on these to control their unruly offspring. As soon as offspring have sprung off to school, they exchange Nanny for au pair if lucky enough to have big enough house with spare room. My frend Hazel has had thousands of au pairs, only one or two of whom cld speak more than three werds of English, so she always found them V. UNCOSY. My mother has spent her life threatening to get nannies and au pairs for us, but she has never had the money, or the space.

Being a V. Paranoid and suspicious person, I always expect nannies to be like Bette Davis in those old horror movies where the nice smiling mummy figure turns out to be evil scheming ghoul Etck, but I think good nannies and au pairs may be a lot more fun than parents for some kids. They don't get so wound up about you and are V. Keen to watch telly, gossip with pals Etck instead of nagging you. Also they have V. cosy phrases like 'You're not the only pebble on the beach' Etck which put you in yr place without putting you DOWN . . .

NEIGHBOURS

If lucky enough to have nice neighbours, they are a boon for Teenage Worriers. They will let you in if you have forgotten yr key, feed yr cat if you have forgotten that too Etck. We drew the line at Mrs Snivel down the road, when she broke a whole lot of neighbour-type rules at once and used our phone to ring Australia for five hours. But all we did was decline use of our phone, which since it's usually cut off anyway was no big thing. We still let her have a thimbleful of milk now and again — and she does the same for us.

I get all the sweeties

ONLY CHILDREN

Only children are sometimes thought to be lonely children. This is cos their parents usually feel V. Guilty about them, trying to get them to have loads of frendz they don't want Etck. In fact, only children are V. Lucky in opinion of El Chubb, as they have more space, clothes Etck, than the rest of us. They also make V. Good frendz as they have more time to give to their frendz, rather than having nagging siblings demanding stuff from them. We are all lonely islands spinning in space, after all, are we not? Touched occasionally by the poetry in another soul, only to be whisked again into the abyss Etck . . .

ORPHANS

However much Yr Parents may Drive You Nutz, it's hard to imagine life without them. Orphans have to face up to this. The TV news is full of stories from parts of the world in which V. Cruel people are creating this situation every day, and you try to imagine what it must be like to be those children, holding each others' hands or the hands of adults they hardly know, and wondering what is going to happen to them. In rare circumstances, because of accidents or illness, this may happen also to children otherwise living much better lives. It prob goes to show that, rich or poor, being an orphan is V. Tough All Round.

We all need to feel loved, and parents, good ones and bad, are better at doing this than most of the alternatives. But, if you are lucky, there are also other Lurveing Members of Yr Family, and friends who know you and Lurve You. They can make it easier to do what seems hard at first – to look out at all the potentially wonderful things the world has to offer, and know that you can find other people to lurve, who will lurve you, too.

I think, perhaps, that if something V. Terrible happens to you like this, you can sometimes think that Lurve is no good because it can go away. Call me old-fashioned, Teenage Worriers, but I will never believe this, I hope.

OVER-PROTECTIVENESS

It may be a V. hard werld in which to bring up infant, junior and Teenage Worriers, but those poor kids like *moi* who were prevented from seeing '12' films until they were fourteen because it might frighten their little brothers or warp their minds Etck are at a distinct disadvantage in
  a) the playground.
  b) the cruel world.

P ARENTS

Parents, whether together, single, step, or divorced come in basic types:

Ideal
Tall, dashing father, miraculously wealthy and yet with endless time to spare for his offspring. He is the dad flying the kite on the heath, bouncing his toddler on his back-pack, offering to run your frendz

home when the last bus has gone Etck. Always checks where you're going in cheerful breezy free'n'easy way. Makes sure he knows who you're with, but never bangs on about who you shouldn't be with. Tells you all he can, helps you all he can, but never says *I told you so* . . . Is married to tall dashing mother, with ever-smiling rosy cheeks, neither glam nor frumpy, who loves her interesting yet not at all demanding work, and is always ready to drop it at an instant because she loves you so much more. These two run the ideal home, wafting with niffs of maple syrup, freshly squeezed oranges, crackling fires Etck. They do not exist on planet Earth, but then perhaps neither does the purrfect teenager . . .

Demanding

These parents are always on your back: *Have you done homework/piano practice/emptied rubbish/tidied your room/ written your thank-you letters/rung your gran/gone to your tennis lesson? If so, why aren't you reading a book instead of watching the telly? Can't you think of anything useful to do with your time? Haven't you got a brain between your ears? You used to be so good at drawing/ballet/ needlework/ice skating, why have you stopped all that?* Or: *Why are you so interested in needlework/football/ reading? Why don't you hang out more with other kids your age?* Etck. Whatever you are doing, as far as these guys are concerned, it shld be something else. Or else you shld be doing it better, or more. This

type is summed up in scary werds of Hazel's dad:
She once told him: 'I'm doing my best', to which he
replied 'Your best isn't good enough.'

TIPS/HINTS: Always try to talk first, and explain
it makes you feel bad, glumey, a failure Etck, to be
nagged all time. Yr parent is V. Likely to love you,
or at least to think they do, so a small discussion
about love (see LOVE) might make them guilty. If
you really think it's impossible to please your folks,
it could be worth age-olde technique of
administering their own medicine. Ask why they
don't earn more, frinstance, or have as big a car as
the neighbours, or why they're not Prime Minister,
Hollywood director Etck. Make sure you do this in
sweet, honeyed tones of reason, not as long whinge.
They will, of course, go Nutz (sometimes followed
by chastened reason) but don't blame *moi* if this
backfires.

Teacher-types

Sometimes this type actually is a teacher in their
working life, but they don't have to be. They just
see it as their job to teach YOU. They are usually V.
sad not to have done more with their own lives, and
are V. keen to make every experience a 'learning
experience' for their lurved offspring, viz: you are
having nice quiet game of *Cluedo* and they lecture
you on complexities of legal system Etck.

HINTS: Own medicine technique. Tell yr parent
in earnest and minute detail, every single thing you

know about something V. dull and obscure (make sure it is the thing they will find least interesting in whole world). You will find it V. boring learning all this and will have to pour over pages of dense medical tome, encyclopaedia Etck but it shld pay dividends.

65

Over-Protective

They will stop you crossing road alone until you have yr own driving license and can prove you know what a car indicator is. You see them anxiously lurking about outside secondary schools wondering if their child is hanging out with right types, whether road surface is treacherous, streetlighting is broken Etck. It is V. Nice to know they DO care, but they need to know how much Worry they cause their poor teenagers, viz: if poor teenager misses bus she has visions of frantick mother dialling 999, sueing bus company for negligence Etck. Also, if you have been told to take care all yr life you are bound to be V. Worried about what it is you are supposed to take care OF. It is not a way to boost confidence.

HINTS/TIPS: Point out lack of confidence above. If this fails, just do the same to them. Insist on knowing exactly what they are doing every second, having all their phone numbers if they are at dinner. Make sure your mum is always wrapped up in that lovely beige, lumpy cardigan you bought her from the charity shop, expecially for this purpose ('I know it smells a bit, Mum, but it's really warm'). Only allow her to take it off during month of August.

TAKE CARE

Mind the TRAFFIC

Be CAREFUL

DON'T talk to STRANGERS

We hear this all our lives. No wonder we're Nervous wrecks...

Embarrassing

Usually the most embarrassing parents are the ones
who try to be ever-young and your frend. They wear
V. Short skirts (and that's just the Dads) and want
to come to parties Etck with you. This must be
nipped in bud V. Kwick. They play music V. Loud,
sing in supermarkets, want to come to parties with
you. Yeeech. Of course, if you have a V. V. Young
single Mum who had you when she was fifteen, this
cld be OK. But only just. She shld be living her life,
not yours.

TIPS/HINTS: Tell Mum/Dad that you Like to be
Alone sometimes . . .

Don't-Care, Never-There

Anyone worrying about over-protective parents
might like to swop with the offspring of Don't-
Care-Never-There types. One week and you'll be
scuttling home to yr oppressive nest. Don't-Cares
come in two distinct types: the V. V. Busy
successful ones who are more interested in
networking with their posh business or arty type
pals than in the tortured agonies of Yr Sole
. . .OR . . . slobbish types who sit in front of TV,
computer, bottle of booze, deaf to any world except
that inside their own heads. They usually feel a
Failure themselves, so are unlikely to give any Lurve
or confidence to You.

TIPS/HINTS: Try telling them how you feel. See
if you can come to some sort of deal, like: having

Do I HAVE to smoke, Dad?

YUK

one evening when you actually talk to each other.
They may respond.

Over-Permissive

Teenage Worriers who love to complain about their
unkind parents who won't let them snort coke,
dance all night, have wild orgies Etck might like to
swap places with offspring of this lot. Nothing cld
be werse than V. over-permissive parents who set
NO BOUNDARIES. If there are NO
BOUNDARIES and yr parents let you do
everything, how can you be a whingeing rebel? Of
course, just like the animals in *Animal Farm*, it is
possible for Teenagers to do what they like,
whatever their folks say. Short of a ball and chain,
how can they stop you? But what some parents don't
know is that it can be fun being stopped. You want
an excuse not to go out doing scary, painful,
damaging things (as well as being allowed to do
lurvely, lush, naughty things). And these kinds of
parents are just too selfish to give it to you. They
love to boast about all the drugs they did themselves
centuries ago in the 70s before all their brain cells
died off, the wild times they had, how yr only young
once, it's your life, it's up to you Etck Etck. Closer
questioning of this type often reveals they only took
small hash cookie once and fainted, when they were
twenty-three. Remind them you are only 15 Etck
and too young to die.

69

Single

Now almost as common as married parents, so no need to feel you stick out like sore thumb and need years of V. Expensive therapy Etck to overcome trauma of:

a) Yr parents being unmarried.

b) Them being divorced.

c) Only ever knowing one of yr parents.

Life is pretty hard for single parents, as they have to earn a living, or fill in humiliating forms Etck to claim measly pittance, and they also have to provide all the love and food and washing Etck. If I were one, I know this wld make me have a shorter fuse and be more grumpy Etck, with my offspring. Unhappiness is what makes people bad-tempered, usually. If yr parent is V. Grumpy, why not ask them why they are so unhappy and why they are taking it out on you? This will make them think (we hope).

Pets

At last! I get a mention

Pets, expecially cats (Rover might be reading this) can be V. Good Company for Teenage Worriers, because they Share Yr Pain with long, deep soulful looks. The cats in the Chubb household are chalk and cheese. Rover is Old, flea-bitten, ratty, demanding and adorable. Kitty is V. Cute to look at and everyone goes *aaaaaaaaah* but she spits and

scratches and wees on yr lap. I am V. Sick of everyone paying more attention to Kitty and neglecting Rover, faithful companion of my childhood Etck. I will never abandon her despite fact that I sneeze forty-five times each morning before I even put foot out of bed cos she insists on sharing my pillow.

PHONE

V. Big source of quarrels as someone always on it when you want it.

In El Chubb's dream dwelling, every Teenage Worrier has their own private direct telephone line or mobile, subsidised by the Govt to encourage you to be a Consumer in Later Telephone Life. How else are we to communicate in Soulless Yooniverse? One V. Good thing about Over-protective parents is that they are starting to get their kiddies mobile phones. Heh! Heh! Sadly, these come complete with mobile phone bills, so you are only allowed to use them in emergencies anyway. I am currently too scared to have one in case I get mugged for it, but I spect they'll soon be cheaper than packet of fruit gums to encourage users, and therefore of less interest to muggers than the laces of Yr Trainers.

QUARRELS SLAM! ARG! BANG! C-R-A-S-H

Just as it's a baby's job to cry, it's a family's job to fight. This does not make crying or fighting any more enjoyable for the people who have to listen to it, which is why you shld respect
    a) yr neighbours and
    b) yr family as far as is yumanly possible, by
KEEPING THE VOLUME DOWN.

NB All fights are founded on one basic principle, although they take many different and subtle (and not-so-subtle) forms. This principle can be summed up in ye famous werds that echo through every cheery household, from high-rise flat to lowly cottage throughout ye lande. They are the three simple werds: *IT'S NOT FAIR*.

Let's run through one or two of Delia Chubbe's fighting recipes to see how these harmless-sounding werds emerge . . .

Usual start: one family member gets computer, sports top, dosh, that other family member wld V.

72

Badly like. Cries of: *IT'S NOT FAIR* ensue, with particular whingeing drawly note on last bit of 'fair', so werd goes high up into aaaaiiiir. Many of you nasty Teenage Worriers with younger siblings will leer at reading this page and rush to shove it in their face. However, take heed: it is no fun being youngest cos nothing is EVER fair. Older kids get to stay up longer, go out more, get more stuff of all kinds. Only answer is, 'Your turn will come.'

Now and then, *IT'S NOT FAIR* will be whined by older sibling. This is because being oldest is never fair either: you get to do homework, chores, Nobody Cares, while younger one gets all the cuddles, soft toys, cries of 'He's only little' Etck Etck. What is V. Not fair about being oldest, is, you are supposed to know better, and not cry *IT'S NOT FAIR*. You are supposed to be Grown-up, take it on chin Etck. The kind of examples our elders show us as spread over tabloids every day show none of them learnt how to button their lip and behave either. BUT, dearest reader, that does not mean we can't try.

One thing Teenage Worriers have got to learn: Life *Isn't* Fair. *IT'S NOT FAIR* that you live near nice skule and boy down road can't get in. *IT'S NOT FAIR* that you have a roof over yr head and gurl in cardboard box doesn't even have lid. If you want to get even more guilty (I lurve a bit of guilt . . . heh, heh, writhe), then try this one: *IT'S NOT FAIR* that you've got clean drinking water and electricity and

← Four
occupants

IT'S NOT FAIR

← Eight
occupants

← Ten
occupants

IT'S NOT FAIR

← Twelve
occupants

IT'S NOT FAIR

vast portions of world are dying for lack of same . . .

The mission of El Chubb is to make Life as fair as poss. Wld only Fair thing be to issue each child with regulation dosh, clothes, sweeties Etck at exactly the same time? Or wld this make life V. DULL AND UNREWARDING?

Rooms

Tragickally, many of us spoilt middle-class teenage worriers were brought up with dolls' houses which contained vast numbers of rumes in which we could exercise our imaginations re wild wallpaper Etck. Real Life is different. I only know one actual house which has the *Cluedo*-style stuff of separate kitchen, dining room and drawing room. And even that house is short of a ballroom and library.

Rule one: however big your home is, one of your caring adults will always say: 'If only we had another room'. This imaginary room is for a study, or a spare bedroom. If they have any cash to slosh around, adults like to slosh it on completely ludicrous events like conservatories or kitchen extensions instead of buying their needy children interesting items like designer trainers, sports tops, game consoles Etck. The latter are too expensive, although a fractional price of the former. Weird.

Rule two: if money tight, then home improvements are effected by member of household.

In our case this means living without any walls or floors for months and sometimes years at a time. Worst of these is half-painted rooms.

ROYAL FAMILY

It is essential in the view of radical El Chubb that we retain ye royal family. They provide deep lessons for ye nation for, despite having all the rooms they cld want, plus ponies, videos, dosh Etck, they do not seem to be completely happy . . .

SISTERS

It is a V. Big tragedy for El Chubb that she has no sisters. I dream of lying in bed at night gossiping in Jane Austen style to my blood relations and soulmates about all the young soldiers, vicars, bums Etck that we might be getting off with. How we wld giggle and scheme! Sigh . . .

STEP-PARENTS

However bad thingz get between Adored Parents, I find it hard to imagine one of them being Somebody Else. However, I know from my Frendz that this not only happens, but can be purrfectly OK if the right people are involved. Nice people are nice people everywhere, and if they're nice to you and seem To Care, you usually respond in the end, even if they're replacing one of the people you thought would be part of yr homelife for ever, and thought they never could be Nice because they got off with Yr Mum/Dad and Broke Yr Werld In Two.

This is prob the TRUE meaning of 'step parent'.

TRADITION

Family traditions can range from V. Eccentric (like always calling yr Father 'Batface' or dancing on urban wasteland wearing nothing but wode on Midsummers Day) to V. Traditional, like having to observe high-days and holidays that have gone back generations, eg: fasting at Ramadan, never cutting hair if you're a boy Sikh, knowing you'll shave it all off one day if you're a gurl Hassidic Jew, Etck Etck. Whatever our culture, it is V. Good to try to understand its roots and reasons Etck, and not assume something else is better just cos it seems easier, or more fun at the time. White Western culture is often attacked for being rootless and without true vision (of God, Spiritual life, Etck) so if you come from a family that does have a sense of such things, you might just be better off than those of us floating around clutching at straws Etck for the Big Meaning. Of course, there are many meanings, and we all, eventually, have to find our own. Traditions can be useful for showing a path either to go down, or as you get to think more about the world, to reject. Either way, traditions can be V. Comforting and we all need them. And all families, of all kinds, need . . .

TREATS

My mother has touching faith in outings as a time for Family-bonding but I must admit I cannot remember any of them happening without an argument, viz: last time we went to zoo I was in V. Animal Rights mode and V. grumpy about living conditions, cages, Etck.

Only one way, in humble opinion of El Chubb, to make family outings a time of happiness, harmony Etck. And that's to allow everybody to choose their fave destination and all go separately since otherwise you will never agree. Sadly, this V. Unfair on Benjy-type younger sibling who's not yet able to cross road alone Etck and therefore has to tag along to the *Wonderful Werld of Butterflies* whether he likes it or not. Sensible tomes will recommend each member gets to choose one outing and everyone goes on it. In our family this wld mean five outings a year which is pushing ye finances somewhat as we are lucky if we get to go to a theme park once a decade.

Tv

Centuries ago when my mother was growing up, adults used to whinge on about how TV wld ruin children's eyesight, lives, brains Etck. Now it is V. difficult for  many Teenage Worriers to prise their afflicted parents away from the box themselves, where they insist on watching game shows for middle-aged worriers instead of Important Searing documentaries or V. Important music and comedy shows. TVs in every room is only answer, though I gather that owing to V. Bad Artistick decline in telly programmes, fewer people are actually watching...

Uncles

Mysterious types who loom at Christmas, hopefully waving a tenner.

NB There are Teenage Worriers who have lots of uncles which is sometimes a name for their naughty mothers' boyfrendz. This also applies to flocks of 'aunties', ahem.

'UNUSUAL'

Although families have always been a grate melting pot of V. Different types of people, you cld still be forgiven for thinking you are 'unusual' if your folks are from different cultures, mixed race, disabled, V. Old, gay, Etck Etck. So let's take these one by one:

We must make ALLOWANCES for Herbert. He's from a very UNUSUAL background...

?

...Ten generations of blond, blue eyed six footers

Poor lad

Different cultures
There are V. V. Few people who are British in the sense that every single one of their ancestors was born and bred here. We are all African if you look

back to first human beings. Even so, we live in a racist culture and different groups of people have different beliefs and customs, so sometimes, however much you know it is silly, you may find it hard to 'fit in'. If you come from a V. traditional Asian or Jewish background frinstance, you may feel it is V. Unfair that other kids have more freedom than you. This is particularly true if, say, yr folks came here when you were a baby and have golden memories of their homeland, where gurlz behaved V. Nicely, so they think. The homeland's changed too, as an Indian mate of mine found when she went to visit there (dressed in a sari) and found all the other gurlz in jeans! Staying in touch with yr roots and culture is V. Important, though, and you have to get yr parents to understand the balance as much as poss.

Mixed Race

If one of yr folks is 'black' and the other 'white' (or, as L. Chubb prefers to call it, 'brown' or 'beige') then you may feel you don't fit in. Course you do. We are all different tones of beige, in fact, from dark to light. We are also (see above) all mixed race, so if anyone gets at you, just tell them we're all Africans at heart. Also,

All These Teenage Women are MIXED RACE

diversity means strength. One of the reasons incest is taboo is that in-breeding causes weakness, so the more different kinds of people who went into making the One-and-Only You, the better.

Disabled

If yr folks can't see, or hear, or walk, you will have a V. Different experience from most of us, and so will they. Often kids from parents with disabilities are much more adventurous and independent than most, cos they have had to be eyes and ears and legs for someone else. You prob feel V. Proud of yr folks, but if you are having a hard time or having to do too much, you cld contact a carers' organisation. This also goes for anyone whose parents are ill.

Gay

Since lots of people are gay, lots of gay people are bound to end up as parents. And they will be just as good, or just as bad, at it as anyone else. They cld feel under more pressure though, and so cld you, as the werld is cruel and kids are V. conservative. Try to forget all that rubbish in the tabloids about lesbian mums and gay dads which is about as stupid as the chants you used to get in the infants playground – remember, whichever boat you are in, there is always someone else in the same boat, and there are lots of organizations nowadays who you can ring up and go to talk to if you feel that you have no-one to share yr worries with.

V. Old

By the time you are a Teenage Worrier, yr parents
will seem V. Old even if they had you when they
were fifteen. Parents just seem to blur into each
other. Now mums seem to be having babies at 60, you
can bet there's always someone with a parent older
than yours, anyway. The real root of fear about having
older parents is that they might die. It is sad but true
that we all face banana sometime, but since the
average age for this is creeping up all the time, it is
unlikely yr folks will pop off before you are an adult,
even if they had you at 60, so try to put this Worry on
the back-burner.

Victims

Who is the whinger in your family? There is always
one who carries the merry family game of *It's Not Fair*
to gargantuan dimensions, so that they are NEVER
happy, but always moaning and droning on about what
a V. Hard lot Mother Nature, the werld and werst of
all, their ungrateful family has loaded them down with.

Real victims, though, who are being sexually
mentally or physically abused, often don't whinge or
even complain at all. This makes me feel V. Guilty
when I think of it. There is apparently a syndrome in
some abusive families where all the kids are treated fine
except one. There was one case I read of where the
youngest child was actually kept in a chicken coop,

while everyone else was beautifully looked after. These are scary stories, but if you know anyone who is being terribly treated like this, or if you are yourself, it is V. Important to get help. Do not suffer in silence!!!!!!!!!!

Violence

← See numbers at end of buke

Much is written in ye tabloid newspapers about footballers and TV stars who beat up their wives. If this is going on in yr house, you really shld get help. Less is written about mental violence, which is harder to prove. You can be beaten up emotionally and psychologically, but there are no bruises to show the police. If either of yr folks is alcoholic, frinstance, this is V. Likely to be going on. Just because they aren't actually hitting you, doesn't mean they aren't hurting you. There are places to ring for children of alcoholics or other verbally or mentally abusive parents.

Weddings

BOING

My Only Father refuses to attend weddings on principle as V. Borgwoise, decadent occasions for people to overspend, make promises they can't keep Etck . . . I have related my horrible experience at being bridesmaid in other tomes, but the general horror of family weddings still lurks over *moi*. I can't face thought of finding right clothes, suitable grimace on mug for hours Etck. I will not attend wedding again. Obvious exception for own, to Daniel . . . and wld also go if my parents ever bothered to get married. Huh.

X MAS

Have to say I V. Much hate this spelling for V. Nice werd 'Christmas', but couldn't think what else to put under 'X' and am firm and dewy-eyed believer in all celebrations. So whatever religion you are, each family has its own version of a feast day. Substitute your own favourite one here. For *moi*, Christmas is a time for ye family to come together in love and peace, ponder ye true meaning of life, sing carols round noble tree Etck. Much has been written about materialism, decline of True Spiritual meanings of season Etck, but El Chubb thinks that Teenage Worriers are ye grate supporters of Christmas. It is the one day you can avoid being nagged about homework as yr parent is too busy burning turkey Etck.

Y ELLING

Yelling is a V. Good way of proving that the same sound is experienced differently by different people.

Let us take, frinstance, a normal Yell of, say, ten decibels as recorded by the El Chubb Impartiality Recording Mechanism. Let's say it is the yell of a normal mother at her normal daughter. This same yell will be heard at twenty zillion decibels by daughter, but her mother will hear it as a reasonable request in a moderate, if firm, voice.

Now let us take the purrfectly normal yell of a daughter at her mother (Impertinence at eighty zillion decibels as heard by mother, but a reasonable refusal as heard by daughter).

This startling insight can be used on many occasions and if it is the only pearl of wisdom in this little tome, then it is werth the cover price, is it not, dear fellow Worriers? If only we could learn to put ourselves in the place of others and see werld through their eyes. Sigh.

Zoos

Aha! You thought the Zoo was somewhere you went to watch the cuddly python and to lament Humanity's relationship to grate Animal Kingdom, didn't you? But, no. The family is a zoo, and each member an animal. Have fun deciding which member of your family is which animal. A lickle cuddly squirrel? (Rats with nice tails, says my horrible father). A busy buzzing bee? (No chance in this house). A Noble Lion (Ashley, sigh). Your view of the animal kingdom and yr family may well change as you progress . . . according to the Chinese calendar I think I was born in the year of the Rat, f'rinstance — must check, cos rats are actually V. Intelligent and caring but have, um, different aims than humanity's.

Have unpleasant feeling that I wld look
like THIS if transformed into animal.
Or THIS

Wonder if I have probs with Inner Self?

ENDPIECE

And now, dear reader, we end our brief survey of the Family, with all its many trials, tribulations, ups, downs, joys, woes (get on with it – Ed), marred only by the sinking feeling that I have but skimmed the tip of the iceberg and hardly scratched the surface of all the many variations of glume that may beset you in struggling with yr family. Cruel truth is, that although each family is different, we are all in same boat when it comes to choice: you can choose your frendz, you may even be lucky enough to choose yr work, or where to live, when you grow up, but you have to make the best of whatever you've got, familywise, until you leave home. So, unless they are cruel, try to be kind to your poor old family. Nobody's purrfect, not even you.

And we ask ourselves, does the purrfect Family exist?

My answer, dearest reader, is yes, briefly, for little moments. These are worth treasuring in yr soul Etck. You might like to use them in dim distant future when creating yr own family.

Who knows? You might make a better job of it . . .

Yrs truly (heading for convent and life of quiet contemplation in order to avoid V. Difficult task of compromising high ideals and getting on with real people like relatives)

Letty Chubb

HELP!

Useful addresses/telephone numbers

Childline
Freephone 0800 1111
A confidential free 24 hour phone line for children in trouble or danger.

National Stepfamily Association
0171 209 2460
   (general enquiries)
0990 168 388
   (confidential helpline)
Advice for anyone on any issue related to being part of a stepfamily.

'Who Cares?' Trust
0171 251 3117
Run by and for young people in care, aiming to make life better for them.

Youth Access
0181 772 9900
Details of young people's counsellors throughout the country.

Adoption/tracing your birth parents
Essential to have counselling before attempting this.
At 18 (17 in Scotland) you can obtain your original birth certificate and sign a contact register by writing for an application form to:
The General Register Office, Smedley Hydro, Trafalgar Road, Birkdale, Southport, Merseyside PB8 2HH

NABS
0171 247 0617
For anyone who has recently suffered the bereavement of a family member. If a brother or sister, ask for SIBS.